COOL CAREERS WITHOUT COLLEGE FOR
PEOPLE
WHO LOVE
MOVEMENT

COOL CAREERS WITHOUT COLLEGE FOR PEOPLE WHO LOVE MOVEMENT

NICOLE FLENDER

The Rosen Publishing Group, Inc.

New York

For Marc, Pauline, and Timothée

Published in 2002 by The Rosen Publishing Group, Inc.
29 East 21st Street, New York, N. Y. 10010

First Edition

Library of Congress Cataloging-in-Publication Data

Flender, Nicole.
Cool careers without college for people who love movement / Nicole Flender.— 1st ed.
p. cm. — (Cool careers without college)
Includes bibliographical references (p.) and index.
Summary: A reference guide providing information about careers in dance, exercise, sports coaching, physical fitness instruction, and other fields involving movement.
ISBN 0-8239-3505-1 (lib. bg.)
1. Physical education and training—Vocational guidance—United States—Juvenile literature. 2. Dance—Vocational guidance—United States—Juvenile literature. [1. Physical education and training—Vocational guidance. 2. Dance—Vocational guidance. 3. Vocational guidance.] I. Title. II. Series.
GV341.5 .F54 2001
331.7'02—dc21

                                                   2001003351

Manufactured in the United States of America

CONTENTS

INTRODUCTION

My nine-year-old daughter is always dancing around the living room to music. It's just something she has to do. If you've been dancing or juggling or playing softball for what seems like forever, a career in movement may be for you.

All of the careers outlined in this book can be embarked on without a college degree. In most circumstances you can have a very successful career without ever going to college. Occasionally, however, you will hit a glass ceiling (invisible barrier) without the college diploma and these cases will be noted.

Some careers, like dancing and gymnastics, require an early start because the muscles, tendons, and ligaments of the body must be stretched and strengthened as they grow. Other careers, such as Pilates instructor, Feldenkrais practitioner, and Alexander Technique teacher, require a lengthy time commitment for training and certification purposes. On the other hand, some other careers require a rather small time commitment. You can be hired as an aerobics instructor by taking some classes, showing enthusiasm for the job, and taking a certification exam given by a reputable fitness association.

Have you always wanted to perform on the stage or in front of large groups of people? There is work in dance companies, musical shows, theme parks, cruise ships, and dance festivals. Outdoor theater festivals are found all over Europe, and if you've developed a clown character and learned some circus skills you can find work and see the world at the same time. It is possible to audition for many of the well-known circuses. These days it is even possible to break into one of the family-dominated highly skilled areas (trapeze, tightrope, dangerous animal acts) if you are well trained in that area.

If you like working one on one with people, you might consider one of the body-mind disciplines covered in this book. Individuals study Pilates, Feldenkrais, and Alexander Technique to increase flexibility and strength, correct posture and release tension, and reverse the effects of debilitating illnesses. Personal trainers work with people to establish an individual workout regimen.

Teaching classes can be like performing because everyone is focused on you. Whether it's dance, yoga, or aerobics, you will have to create the class program from start to finish, designing steps and choreography that are appropriate to the level you are teaching. This might lead you to start doing choreography for shows.

Most work with children takes place in private dance studios. You can find freelance work in the public school system as a teaching artist. There is a strong movement to put the arts back in education, and there are full-time positions for dance and movement teachers. There is work to be found with babies and seniors, too.

Team sports are a very popular way for kids to get exercise—in school, after school, and on the weekends. A good coach can be a kid's (not to mention a parent's) hero. The various martial arts have taken off in this country over the past twenty years, and students of all ages are looking for good teachers.

Unless you are a member of a company or of a circus, paid with a weekly salary, you will be a freelancer. Freelancers enjoy the freedom of arranging their own schedules but suffer the uncertainty of a steady paycheck. As you read through these pages, you might want to consider putting several jobs together: performing, teaching, and even starting your own business.

CONCERT DANCER

Professionals in a dance company perform concert dance. They learn dances choreographed by the director of the company or a guest choreographer. The repertoire, or list of dances, is usually rotated during a company's season so there are several different programs to see and more than one chance to see a certain dance. The most common

types of concert work are ballet and modern dance. Other disciplines, such as tap dancing, ballroom dancing, and jazz dancing, are occasionally presented in concert form.

Ballet dancing is very rigorous and requires a lot of discipline. Usually female dancers start training seriously at eight or nine years of age. Boys can start a little later. By the age of twelve, serious students take at least one class a day, five or six days a week. There are exceptions where late starters have wonderful careers. Ballet requires tremendous flexibility, a perfect turnout, and beautifully pointed feet. Older children will start to lose these qualities unless a conscious effort is made to work on them. It should be noted that ballet is a wonderful preparation for all kinds of dance; indeed it is the basis on which all other techniques are built. Ballet stresses technique, alignment, control, and poise, and should be studied by everyone who wants to dance professionally.

Classical ballet comes from the Italian and French court dances of the fifteenth century. Court dancing reached its peak under the French king Louis XIV, and ballet terminology today is universally French. By the late 1600s, professional dancing began to replace court dancing.

A class of ballet students practices dance fundamentals.

In the early twentieth century, Lincoln Kirstein, a scholar and great friend of the dance, invited Russian-born George Balanchine to America. In 1934 they established the School of American Ballet (SAB), and in 1946 the school's dance company, the New York City Ballet, was born. It is thanks to "Mr. B" that classical ballet as we know it exists in this country. Protégées of Balanchine and former members of the company run many companies and affiliated schools nationwide.

Some children start training at large schools when they are very young. Others train at small studios and then spend summers at larger schools in big cities. There is good training all over but it is your job to find it. See if you can observe a class at a school or ask someone who knows something about ballet if you are not sure. Often a former professional dancer will open a school back in his or her hometown. If he or she has danced with a reputable company for many years, chances are he or she will be a good teacher. Some wonderful companies with affiliated schools include Pacific Northwest Ballet, Miami City Ballet, and the National Ballet of Canada.

Female dancers usually begin pointe study, or toe work, after three years of training but not before eleven or twelve years of age. By the age of sixteen, a ballet hopeful should be taking at least two classes a day. Students at this level

A group of young girls watch as their classmate goes through a new routine. They will each get a turn to show their instructor what they have learned.

study pointe work, partnering with male dancers, and variations. At this advanced level you may be asked to join the affiliated company of the school where you are training or another company, or you may start auditioning. A ballet audition usually consists of a class where you are judged by the managers of the company. Some dancers may be hired right away. Others may be put "on file" to be considered again at a later date.

Modern dance began in America in the early twentieth century, as a reaction to ballet. Many dancers find modern

In addition to technical exercises, dancers have to keep in shape with regular exercises that build strength, endurance, and flexibility.

dance less rigid in structure and more tolerant of imperfect bodies. Exact turnout is not required, nor is painful training of the foot on pointe. Modern dancers perform barefoot and work with gravity instead of against it. In fact, the use of falls is quite common in modern dance. Supporting this free-form type of movement, many modern dance choreographers make multidimensional use of space. In ballet the music often underscores the rhythm of the dance movement. In modern dance the music can work counter to or independently of the movement.

Much of modern dance is codified. Contract and release, fall and recovery are a couple of standard exercises. Among the pioneers of modern dance were Ted Shawn and Ruth St. Denis. Their dance retreat, Jacob's Pillow, paved the way for choreographers and dancers Martha Graham, Charles Weidman, and Doris Humphrey. Jacob's Pillow still exists as a well-respected summer festival site where all styles of dance are presented.

There are many disciples of former and current great modern dancers who have formed their own companies and developed their own styles. Paul Taylor was a longtime Martha Graham dancer, and his company and school are world-renowned today. David Parsons is a Paul Taylor disciple who now has a very young and enthusiastic company of his own.

A Day in the Life of a Ballet Dancer

At eighteen Lesleh Gage is an advanced student at the School of American Ballet. She moved to New York from Texas three years ago and has been living in the dorm at SAB. She takes two classes a day in addition to Pilates class three times a week. Because her dance schedule is so demanding, she is finishing up high school on correspondence. She will be going to Miami City Ballet this summer. Could a position in that company be far off?

If a company belongs to the American Guild of Musical Artists (AGMA) it gives union contracts to its members. Minimum salaries exist for apprentice, ensemble soloist, and principal positions if you are in a large company. A first year corps de ballet member of the New York City Ballet makes $858 per week. A soloist makes $1,723 per week, and principal dancers can negotiate even higher. At the smaller company of Ballet Hispanico, salaries are figured by the number of years the dancer has been with the company. An apprentice makes $263, a first-year member $487, and a twenty-year member $935. At the beginning of your dance career, you may find yourself performing in small spaces for little or no money. Not every job has to be union.

The competition to get a job as a dancer is fierce. There are always more dancers than jobs. But as dancers retire and more jobs are created work becomes available. The median wage for a dancer is less than $20,000 a year, according to Department of Labor statistics. Given the hard work and uncertain pay, dancing is something you must love to do.

FOR MORE INFORMATION

ORGANIZATIONS

American Guild of Musical Artists
1727 Broadway
New York, NY 10019
(212) 265-3687
Web site: http://www.musicalartists.org

Gus Giordano Jazz Dance Center
614 Davis Street
Evanston, IL 60201
(847) 866-9228
A great place to study jazz dance, founded by Gus Giordano, one of the masters.

The Limón Institute

Limón Dance Company
611 Broadway, 9th Floor
New York, NY 10012
(212) 777-3353
Web site: http://limon.org
A modern-dance school in the tradition of the wonderful dancer
José Arcadio Limón.

The National Ballet School

105 Maitland Street
Toronto, ON M4Y 1E4
Canada
(416) 964-3780
Web site: http://www.nationalballetschool.org
The professional ballet school of the National Ballet of Canada.

The School of American Ballet

70 Lincoln Plaza
New York, NY 10023
(212) 877-0600
Web site: http://nycballet.com
This is the official ballet school of the New York City Ballet, which
George Balanchine founded with Lincoln Kirstein more than fifty
years ago. It is highly competitive to gain admission and auditions are
conducted routinely all over the country.

WEB SITES

DanceArt.com

http://www.dancepages.com
This Web site lists reputable schools where you can study.

BOOKS

Anderson, Jack. *Ballet and Modern Dance: A Concise History*. Princeton, NJ: Princeton Book Co., 1992.

Garafola, Lynn, and Eric Foner. *Dance for a City: Fifty Years of the New York City Ballet*. New York: Columbia University Press, 1999.

Jones, Mark. *Dancer's Resource*. New York: Watson-Guptill Publications, 1999.

Kuklin, Susan, and Bill T. Jones. *Dance!* New York: Hyperion Press, 1998.

Mitchell, Jack, and Richard Philip. *Alvin Ailey American Dance Theater*: Jack Mitchell Photographs. Kansas City, MO: Andrews & McMeel, 1993.

MAGAZINES

These magazines are full of information on schools, competitions, auditions, and other bits of useful information.

Dance Magazine
111 Myrtle Street, #203
Oakland, CA 94607
(800) 873-9863
(510) 839-6060
Web site: http://www.dancemagazine.com

Dance Spirit
250 West 57th Street, Suite 420
New York, NY 10107
(800) 331-1750
(212) 265-8890
Web site: http://www.dancespirit.com

Stern's Directory
111 Myrtle Street, #203
Oakland, CA 94607
(800) 873-9863
A publication of *Dance Magazine* listing companies and schools in the
United States and Canada.

SHOW
BUSINESS
DANCER

Dancers who decide to go into show business need to be, as the name implies, very business savvy. In concert dance, talent is paramount. In show business, talent is important, but there are other considerations. Are you tall? Are you blonde? Can you do back handsprings? Can you fit into a certain costume?

Dancers in show business perform in Broadway, touring, or local resident shows. The famed Radio City Music Hall Rockettes are show business dancers. Bigger money can be made in film and television work. Good starting places are cruise ships and theme parks, such as Disney World.

As stated in the previous chapter, ballet is the foundation for all types of dance. The show business dancer need not be as proficient as the concert dancer but he or she must be more versatile. Knowledge of jazz, tap, acting, and singing is a must. At a typical Broadway audition, a dancer may be given a ballet or jazz routine to perform, and then be asked to sing part of a song. Initially dancers may be "typed" according to their looks. As each group of four or five dancers performs a combination, a "cut" is made. If there are a hundred dancers at the beginning of an audition, there may be twenty left at the end to be "called back" for another day. The more skills you have, the better; if you can tap on your toes or twirl a baton, you may be needed. In the Broadway revival of *Cabaret*, dancers were hired who could play musical instruments.

The Actors' Equity Association (AEA) covers professional stage work. Producers negotiate periodically with the union to update contracts. The production contract is the top of the line and covers Broadway and first-rate tours. Minimum salary is $1,252 per week. Other contracts

The Rockettes in a scene from the Radio City Music Hall revue *Encore*

include stock and guest artist, where the salary can be as low as $250 per week. The Rockettes are covered by AGVA, the American Guild of Variety Artists. They perform under a negotiated contract as well. Outside of New York the Rockettes make $1,250 per week for their Christmas show. The show is done in New York, Branson, Chicago, Detroit, Nashville, Atlanta, Cincinnati, and Cleveland. Big Hollywood musicals are a thing of the past, but dancers are still used in films such as *Footloose*, *Center Stage*, and *Billy Elliot*. Dancers are also used in commercials. Recent ads for the Gap used many dancers. Anything that is filmed is covered by SAG, the Screen Actors Guild. Minimum salary for a principal dancer is $617 a day for a film and $500 a day for a commercial. Television shows that are taped are covered by AFTRA, the American Federation of Television and Radio Artists. Principal AFTRA minimum salary for a one-hour variety show is $775 a day.

You can find out about auditions for shows through a trade paper called *Backstage*, which also has a subscription Web service at http://www.backstage.com, or through Actors' Equity's Web site at http://www.actorsequity.org. Both of these sources list auditions nationwide. Most auditions take place in New York, although many regional theaters hold additional auditions on site. It is difficult to get a union job without being a union member, and it may help to do some nonunion work and get experience for your

Dancer Ethan Stiefel in *Center Stage*, a movie about the tensions involved in the competition for roles in a ballet company

résumé first. You will need to get a black-and-white glossy photo of yourself, also known as a headshot, to which you staple your résumé. A good headshot can cost $400 and needs to be reproduced professionally for an additional fee.

To get auditions for film, television, and commercials, you need an agent. To get an agent you must demonstrate your skills. Agents attend unpaid showcases and invite performers to audition for them in a studio or an office. Once again, it pays to be versatile. Many people "do rounds," going door-to-door, slipping their photos and

A dancer auditions before judges as other hopefuls wait their turn during a casting call for the Radio City Rockettes at Radio City Music Hall in New York City.

résumés under agents' doors, hoping to be called in for an interview. Dancers like to get commercials and films. If the film or commercial is shown repeatedly or taken to other markets such as cable television or television stations abroad, the dancer receives residuals, or additional payments each time the commercial or film is shown.

It is not uncommon for a Broadway dancer to perform at night and to run around to auditions for other Broadway shows, commercials, and TV shows during the day. If it's a slow day for auditions, he or she may take a couple of dance

> Bebe Neuwirth is the ideal Broadway success story. She trained at the Joffrey Ballet School in New York City and became a replacement in the Broadway production of *A Chorus Line*. Legendary choreographer Bob Fosse chose her for the role of Nikki in the revival of *Sweet Charity*. Her outstanding acting ability earned her the role of Lilith on the television series, *Cheers*. Recently she returned to Broadway to star in the revival of *Chicago*.

classes and a voice lesson. Sometimes dancers become so good at singing and acting that they become true triple threats. These performers become quite sought after and end up doing leading roles such as Peggy Sawyer in *42nd Street* or Cassie in *A Chorus Line*.

Although the possibilities seem endless in show business, it can be a very uncertain way of life. In a dance company, if you do your job, you are guaranteed a certain number of weeks of work a year. If you are in a Broadway show, you could be out of work in a week if the show flops. A show business dancer is always looking for work, always expanding his or her horizons, always adding more things to his or her personal repertoire.

As with concert dance, there is tremendous competition for jobs in show business. The good news is that once you have established a niche with a choreographer, a theater, or a producer, you have a greater chance of being hired by them.

FOR MORE INFORMATION

ORGANIZATIONS

Actors' Equity Association
165 West 46th Street
New York, NY 10036
(212) 869 8530
Web site: http://www.actorsequity.org
Theatrical union representing dancers. Their Web site lists auditions by contract and location. Interesting articles and facts.

American Federation of Television and Radio Artists
National Office—Los Angeles
5757 Wilshire Boulevard, 9th Floor
Los Angeles, CA 90036-3689
(323) 634-8100
Web site: http://www.aftra.com

American Federation of Television and Radio Artists
National Office—New York
260 Madison Avenue

New York, NY 10016-2402
(212) 532-0800
Web site: http://www.aftra.com

American Guild of Variety Artists
184 Fifth Avenue
New York, NY 10036
(212) 675-1003

Canadian Actors' Equity Association
44 Victoria Street
12th Floor
Toronto, ON M5C 3C4
Canada
Web site: http://www.caea.com
The Canadian equivalent of AEA representing choreographers as well. Their Web site lists auditions, workshops, and other employment opportunities.

Screen Actors Guild
National Office
5757 Wilshire Boulevard
Los Angeles, CA 90036
Web site: http://www.sag.com
The Web site lists all agents franchised by the Guild.

BOOKS

Bolin, Bobby. *A Dancer's Manual: A Motivational Guide to Professional Dancing*. Toluca Lake, CA: Rafter Publishing, 1999.

Gottfried, Martin. *All His Jazz: The Life and Death of Bob Fosse*. New York: Da Capo Press, 1998.

Kirkwood, James, Nicolas Dante, Marvin Hamlisch, Edward Kleban, and Michael Bennet. *A Chorus Line: The Book of the Musical*. New York: Applause Theater Book Publications, 1999.

Suskin, Steven. *Opening Night on Broadway*. New York: Schirmer Books, 1990.

MAGAZINES

Backstage **and** *Backstage West* **(available in Los Angeles)**
P.O. Box 5017
Brentwood, TN 37024
(800) 437-3183
Web site: http://www.backstage.com
Lists auditions and casting seminars. Trade papers with valuable articles related to "the business." Their Web site lists auditions by subscription. Very detailed breakdowns of what is required. Articles related to the business.

Ross Reports
P.O. Box 5018
Brentwood, TN 37024
(800) 817-3273
A monthly booklet updating agents and casting directors in New York and Los Angeles.

CHOREOGRAPHER AND DANCE ASSISTANT

A choreographer makes up dance steps for concert dances, musical shows, movies, television shows, parades, and special events. The more styles of dance a choreographer knows, the more work he or she will be able to get. Some choreographers feel comfortable creating dances in one medium. Others switch between live

Famed ballet dancer and choreographer Mikhail Baryshnikov directs ballet dancers during a rehearsal.

stage, television, and film. George Balanchine choreographed Broadway musicals and was also cofounder and artistic director of the New York City Ballet. He choreographed dozens of original ballets that are still being performed by that company and companies all over the world today. Balanchine was such a versatile choreographer that he even choreographed a ballet for the Ringling Bros. and Barnum & Bailey elephants called the "Circus Polka." Lynne Taylor-Corbett has choreographed numerous commercials. She has choreographed for ballet companies and Broadway as well. If you saw the Broadway or touring productions of *Footloose*, you saw her choreography.

Many budding choreographers who are members of a ballet or modern-dance company use members of that company for their choreography. When he or she feels ready, a choreographer may break away and form a company of his or her own. Paul Taylor, founder of a very well-known modern–dance school and company, was a Martha Graham dancer originally. One of Paul's dancers, David Parsons, eventually felt the need to branch out on his own and is now the director of the Parsons Dance Company.

Choreographers for new musical shows are hired based on their expertise. Usually a choreographer has paid his or her dues working on revivals of shows in summer stock, dinner theater, or regional theater. A reputation is built on reviews and compatibility with the other members of the creative team (director and musical director) in addition to the quality of the work. Another way to gain experience is to assist a choreographer. You will be doing a lot of the grunt work (getting coffee, taking notes, standing in for dancers who are getting costume fittings) but it is a great way to get your name known and to build your résumé.

Dance captains keep a musical show in shape after the choreographer leaves. The dance captain watches the show on a regular basis and oversees rehearsals for understudies

Choreographer Arlene Philips leads a company of dancers practicing a new routine.

and new cast members. General cleanup rehearsals for the entire cast are held as well.

If choreography gives you a kick, offer your talents for your local school production. Even elementary schools put on musical plays. Believe it or not, many high schools and junior high schools hire, and pay, professional choreographers. If you show your arts coordinator that you're good, he or she may let you take a crack at the next production. You may not get paid but you may start building your skills and your résumé. Check out your local religious and community centers as well.

Frequently there are ads in the trade paper *Backstage* for choreographers. Beginning jobs may pay only a flat fee of a few hundred dollars. The best way to find work once you have a few shows under your belt is through word of mouth. Remember that people like talent, but they also like someone who is easy to get along with. Be willing to compromise with your artistic colleagues.

It may be of interest to note that you may work for a long time as a choreographer making very little money, but then you may hit it big overnight. The choreographers union, the Society of Stage Directors and Choreographers (SSD&C), requires all of its members to file contracts even if they are working for free! The union guarantees the choreographers' ownership of the

A Tip for You

Veteran dancer Andrea Andresakis got her start as a choreographer at Allenberry Playhouse in Pennsylvania after having performed there in two shows. She recommends that young choreographers get in the studio to work with dancers as often as possible.

material for future paid productions. SSD&C has been able to successfully negotiate contracts with producers. This is called collective bargaining. Salaries on these contracts range from $814 for eight days of rehearsal and a weekly guarantee of $258 on the low end, to an up-front payment of $38,620 and $20,000 a week royalties for a hit Broadway show.

Some growth is expected in this field. It may be hard to find work at first but once you prove yourself and gain professional contacts, colleagues you once knew as a dancer will be competing to be in your show.

FOR MORE INFORMATION

ORGANIZATIONS

Society of Stage Directors and Choreographers (SSD&C)
1501 Broadway
New York, NY 10036
(212) 391-1070
Web site: http://www.ssdc.org
The union of stage directors and choreographers. Guarantees salary on some contracts. Guarantees pension and health on all contracts. Provides information on arts grants.

Stage Directors & Choreographers Foundation
1501 Broadway
New York, NY 10036
(212) 302-5359
A not-for-profit organization with resources to help choreographers network, present work, and find jobs.

BOOKS

Humphrey, Doris. *The Art of Making Dances*. New York: Rinehart, 1959.

Smith-Autard, Jacqueline. *Dance Composition: A Practical Guide for Teachers*. London: Lepus Books, 1976.

4

DANCE TEACHER

Once you've studied dance for a long time and you've done some performing, you may decide to try your hand at teaching. Teachers must enjoy working with young people and have a passion to pass knowledge on to others. In this chapter we will examine what it takes to teach dance in a studio setting.

Dance became popular in this country in the mid-1960s, and interest has been increasing ever since. In addition to the large dance schools like the School of American Ballet, the Martha Graham School, and the Pacific Northwest Ballet School, there are numerous local dancing schools in every large and small town from Maine to California. If you are studying dance now, chances are you are with one of these schools.

For teachers-to-be, a good way to get experience is by teaching part-time while you are still studying or performing. Offer to teach at your dance studio, as an assistant or with young children. Any experience counts on a résumé. If you move to New York, have a professional career, and then decide to become a full-time teacher, you will already have some credits.

If you are a dancer who is lucky enough to land a national tour, take advantage of the free publicity and call local dance schools in each city you visit, with the offer of teaching as a guest artist. Most of the studios' dancers will want to take a class with the cast member of the hit musical or ballet that's in town, and the studio owners will be happy with the extra income. You should be able to make $100 a class for these "master classes." Don't be surprised if the local newspaper comes to cover the event and you get a photo clipping! Meanwhile you're building your résumé.

A dance instructor works with her class during stretching exercises.

There are no formal requirements to teach in a large, company-affiliated school or a local dancing school. Generally teachers are hired based on their professional performing experience, their inclination to teach, and a dance style that is in keeping with the philosophy of the school. Teaching at a local dancing school generally pays between $25 and $75 a class according to your level of experience and the location of the school. In addition to teaching your classes, you may be called upon to choreograph dances for performances and competitions. You will be paid extra for this, although you may get a flat fee instead of an hourly one. Dancers will pay from $300 to $600 for a competition dance. Duets and trios share expenses.

To teach in either a public or private school, you would need to get a bachelor's degree in dance with a certain number of credits in education. Teaching in an academic setting with a teaching license guarantees you a salary with yearly raises, health insurance, and pension benefits. Starting salaries for teachers are anywhere from $30,000 to $45,000 a year. Some public schools invite professional dancers or performing artists to teach dance classes in their school without a degree. These teachers are usually paid by a parents' association or an arts grant. Fees are paid hourly and can range from $25 to $50 an hour for approximately one-hour classes. Various education programs are offered to further the training of teachers for local dance schools

Professional ballet dancer Catalina Bohiltea became injured and was forced to retire from the Hartford Ballet in her mid-20s. She started teaching at local dancing schools in the Connecticut area, and today she is the ballet mistress at Westport's Academy of Dance in Westport, Connecticut. She teaches more than twenty classes a week and choreographs for recitals and competitions. She advises young teachers to work their way up: "Someone teaching for the first time should start with small children and graduate with them from class to class and level to level."

and as performing artists. A list of these programs is given in the directory portion of this chapter.

Many schools have developed on site, after-school dance programs to keep youngsters busy while mom and dad are working. You do not need a college degree to work in these programs, and often you are assigned a high school assistant. Developing your own dance program in an after-school setting can be very rewarding. It's up to you to decide what dance uniforms the children should wear, what syllabus (instructional method) you will use, and when you will put on shows for the parents. Local YMCAs, youth centers, and camps all need dance teachers as well. Send them your photo and résumé.

Tap-dancing little girls and their instructors kick their legs along a barre in a dance studio.

Dancers are performers and should always have a photo—a headshot or a dance pose—attached to their résumés.

Be sure to keep your résumé up-to-date. Tell everyone you know that you're looking for teaching work. Check listings in dance publications, notices on studio boards, and even your local paper. Let friends know you are available to substitute for them. Many schools require teachers to find their own substitutes when they're absent. This is a great way to get your foot in the door. Remember to bring copies of your résumé, a cover letter written to the studio director, and recent recital programs.

It's great to find work close to home, but if you're willing to travel, you'll probably get more teaching contracts. If you're primarily a ballet dancer but can also teach beginner tap and jazz, let your employer know. Additional skills could lead to extra classes and more money. Also, be willing to start as an assistant. The pay may be lower, but it's a good way to establish new contacts and credits. The outlook for getting work as a dance teacher is good.

Your own dance success results from the hard work and support of the many teachers who helped you along the way. As a teacher, you can pass on the tradition to the next generation of ballerinas and tap-dance kids.

FOR MORE INFORMATION

TEACHER TRAINING PROGRAMS

Bill Evans New Mexico Tap Dance Festival
Dance Program
Center for the Arts
University of New Mexico
Web site: http://www.billevansdance.org
Courses for dance teachers in tap technique, styles, and repertory.

Broadway Dance Center
221 West 57th Street, 5th Floor
New York, NY 10019
(800) 357-3525
Web site: http://www.bdcsummerintensive.com
This large New York dance training facility offers seminars for teachers in several dance disciplines.

National Ballet School of Canada
Art and Science of Dance
105 Maitland Street
Toronto, ON M4Y IE5
Canada
(416) 946-3780
Teaches the great ballet traditions with a different concentration each year.

Pacific Northwest Ballet School
Teachers Seminar
301 Mercer Street
Seattle, WA 98109
(206) 441-3579
Web site: http://www.pnb.org
Offers a three-day course with lectures, company class observation, and participation in special dance classes

BOOKS

Lewis, Daniel. *The Illustrated Dance Technique of José Limón*. Hightstown, NJ: Princeton Book Company, 1999.

Roseman, Janet Lynn. *Dance Masters: Interviews with Legends of Dance*. New York: Routledge, 2001.

Schorer, Suki. *Suki Schorer on Balanchine Technique*. New York: Alfred A. Knopf, 1999.

Warren, Gretchen Ward. *The Art of Teaching Ballet: Ten Twentieth-Century Masters*. Gainesville, FL: University Press of Florida, 1996.

White, John. *Teaching Classical Ballet*. Gainesville, FL: University Press of Florida, 1996.

MAGAZINES

Dance Magazine
111 Myrtle Street, #203
Oakland, CA 94607
(800) 873-9863
(510) 839-6060
Web site: http://www.dancemagazine.com
This seventy-year-old magazine has a monthly performance calendar, a "Teacher Talk" column, and a dance school directory. Once a year they host a most inspiring teacher contest. You may list yourself as a teacher in their *Stern's Directory* at no charge.

Dance Teacher
250 West 57th Street, Suite 420
New York, NY 10107
(800) 331-1750
Web site: http://www.dance-teacher.com
A publication that discusses master teachers, schools, injury prevention, and curriculum. Regularly has listings of studios and teacher training programs.

5

FITNESS INSTRUCTOR AND PERSONAL TRAINER

Fitness instructors work with a group of individuals in different kinds of exercise classes, whereas personal trainers work one-on-one with individuals to tailor an exercise regimen to one person's needs. Many fitness instructors lead regular classes in strength training and cardio-vascular exercises such as aerobics, at gyms. Personal trainers work at health clubs, with free weights and various machines, and with clients at their homes or offices.

People go to health clubs to maintain health and fitness. Overweight people go to lose weight and decrease fat. A wide variety of classes are available at health clubs. Aerobics classes get the heart rate up. Considered cardio-vascular exercise, they strengthen your heart and lungs and burn lots of calories. Aerobics classes exist in many forms. Toning classes target the look of the body. In these body-sculpting classes, people do exercises to define abdominal, thigh, buttock, and arm muscles. Often people rush to these classes in the spring thinking they will look great in that new bathing suit by the summer. Stretch class is geared for people who want to improve or maintain flexibility. As we get older, our tendons shorten and tighten. Our movements become slower and we find it increasingly difficult to maintain good posture. Stretch class also helps athletes move in a wide variety of directions. All instructors should incorporate warm-up and cooldown exercises into their classes.

A good fitness instructor should be aware of everyone in his or her class, even if he or she doesn't know everyone on a first-name basis. He or she should also be aware of the average level of the students' physical condition. The idea is to have everyone keep up without the more advanced people becoming bored. Assessment is the key. Find out who has never taken either your class or a similar one

A fitness instructor leads her clients in stretching exercises during an aerobics session.

before, or if anyone is injured. Give clear instructions but don't be tempted to talk too much. If you use music, keep up on the latest trends; repetition can be boring. Give corrections to individuals and to the class. A sense of humor never hurt anyone. When people are working hard and feel they can't go on, jokes and encouragement work wonders.

People go to personal trainers for workout programs that are tailor-made for their needs and goals. Sessions can take place in a health club or at the client's home. Often, at a health club you will help clients become familiar with the various workout machines. Ultimately these clients may become familiar enough with their routines to work out on their own and check in with you when they wish to increase the strength of their program. Clients who want you to come to their homes may prefer to work out in private and may need a trainer's motivation. Either way, a good trainer will listen carefully to the client's expectations and gauge signs of physical stress. Some people complain when they are in pain. Others grin and bear it. Be prepared to answer lots of questions and to write down the various exercises and machines you have used for each client. It's important to keep up-to-date with new research and findings and to be able to assess if the information is applicable to your clients' needs.

Louisiana is currently the only state with legal requirements for fitness trainers, yet it's hard to get a job in a bona fide health club without certifications from one or more of the leading associations listed in the directory section of this chapter. Many fitness instructors turn to personal training as a way to branch out and make more money.

Fitness instructors earn anywhere from $25 to $50 a class depending on geographical location. Personal trainers, in a health club, earn about the same depending on their level of expertise. If you go to clients' homes and are in large demand, you can charge up to $100 an hour. If

Just What Is an Aerobics Class?

Aerobics classes come in a variety of styles:

- **High impact.** Involves a lot of jumping off the floor. Not for the faint of heart!
- **Low impact.** Lots of leg lifts and arm lifts but no jumping.
- **Step.** Sequences of steps on and off a rectangular platform.
- **Spinning.** An energetic, guided workout on a stationary bicycle.
- **Kickboxing.** Incorporates martial arts moves and puts them to music.
- **Funk.** Learn hip, new club dance moves including hip hop.

Members of an aerobics class perform step exercises using a platform.

you maintain a healthy lifestyle, enjoy teaching and motivating others, and have good communication and leadership abilities, this is a great field to get into. According to a recent International Dance Exercise Association (IDEA) poll, there was a 55 percent average growth rate from 1998 to 1999 for fitness instructors and personal trainers. As active baby boomers enter the retirement phase, there will be an increase in the demand for fitness instructors and trainers.

FOR MORE INFORMATION

ORGANIZATIONS

The groups below are widely recognized fitness organizations that provide information on careers in fitness as well as certification exams.

American College of Sports Medicine (ACSM)
401 W. Michigan Street
Indianapolis, IN 46202
(317) 637-9200
Web site: http://www.acsm.org

American Council on Exercise (ACE)
5820 Oberlin Drive, Suite 102
San Diego, CA 92121-3787
(858) 535-8227
(800) 825-3636
Web site: http://www.acefitness.org

National Athletic Trainers' Association (NATA)
2952 Stemmons Freeway
Dallas, TX 75247
(800) 879-6282
(214) 637-6282
Web site: http://www.nata.org

National Dance Exercise Instructor's Association (NDEITA)
5955 Golden Valley Road, Suite 240
Minneapolis, MN 55422
(800) 237-6242
(763) 545-2524
Web site: http://www.ndeita.com
This association incorporates dance movements into its training and
certification requirements.

BOOKS

American College of Sports Medicine. *ACSM's Guidelines for Exercise
Training and Prescription.* Baltimore: Williams & Wilkins, 2000.

Andes, Karen. *The Complete Book of Fitness: Mind, Body, Spirit.* New
York: Crown, 1999.

Baechle, Thomas, and Roger Earle. *Essentials of Strength Training and
Conditioning.* Champaign, IL: Human Kinetics, 2000.

Franks, B. Don, and Edward T. Howley. *Fitness Leaders Handbook*. Champaign, IL: Human Kinetics Publishers, 1998.

Heyward, Vivian. *Advanced Fitness and Exercise Prescription*. Champaign, IL: Human Kinetics, 1997.

Powers, Scott K. *The Essentials of Total Fitness: Exercise, Nutrition, and Wellness*. Needham Heights, MA: Allyn & Bacon, 1997.

MAGAZINES

Health and Fitness Sports Magazine
1502 Augusta, Suite 480
Houston, TX 77057
(713) 552-9991
Web site: http://www.healthandfitnessmag.com

Shape
Web site: http://www.shapemag.com
Available on newsstands. This publication highlights the latest fitness trends and promotes a healthy and fit lifestyle.

6

SPORTS COACH

Until recently, with the formation of the National Council for Accreditation of Coaching Education, coaching a sports activity was highly unregulated in America. In fact, there are currently no laws requiring any kind of coaching education. Some coaching jobs require merely an adequate knowledge of a sport along with an ability to work well with children. Others require CPR and safety certification along with respected coaching certifications in the field. For scholastic sports, a bachelor's or a master's degree is needed since often the coach is also the school's physical education teacher.

Many people start their coaching careers as volunteers. They have gained a certain expertise in soccer, softball, basketball, ice hockey, cheerleading, or some other sport; they enjoy working with young children; and they have leadership abilities. Volunteer positions exist at parks and recreation departments; Boys and Girls Clubs of America; and ad hoc, Sunday-morning, neighborhood games. Various associations exist to help volunteers with teaching skills, sportsmanship, nutrition counseling, and prevention of injuries, and to provide information about the latest equipment. Some associations offer CPR training and safety courses.

Extracurricular youth clubs pay approximately $25 an hour to coaches who train and motivate kids in a team sport. In addition to expert knowledge of your field, you must practice ethical behavior and believe that competitive sports are above all for fitness and fun. Parents want

Volunteering as a coach in a community program for children is a great way to begin a coaching career.

their kids' teams to win. More important, they want their kids to be happy. Playing team sports can give children self-esteem and confidence, even when their teams do not win. It is the coach's job to shout words of encouragement—"Nice job, keep it up!"—and to instill pleasure in the game, regardless of the outcome. This may require resisting parental pressure to win, and even remaining calm and controlled in the face of verbal abuse and criticism. With a good coach, a team quickly becomes a family, and lifelong friendships are formed.

Occasionally you will come across a parent who is so competitive that he or she hurls insults at the other team, speaks impolitely to the coach, or threatens or uses violence against the coach if the team loses or if the child is not used enough in the game. It is important to make clear from the start that you practice good sportsmanship. Many associations publish a code of ethics that you can follow. The state of Massachusetts has endorsed a Sport Parent Code of Conduct, which highlights disciplinary actions for misconduct.

In addition to big team sports such as basketball, ice hockey, and soccer, there are sports such as gymnastics, swimming, and fencing that are practiced in teams and individually. Coaches in these fields can also double as instructors. A coach gets the individual or team ready for

Coaches and instructors need to be good communicators, especially those who work with children.

competition whereas the instructor teaches the fundamentals of the sport.

Jobs as paid coaches and instructors can be found at local YMCAs, after-school programs, youth and recreation centers, preschool gyms, and sports clubs. Most coaching positions are part-time since games and lessons happen on the weekend and after school.

If you love this kind of work and want to devote yourself to it full-time, you will have to get a bachelor's degree from

Americans' Favorite Spectator Sports (Gallup Poll 2001)

Football

Basketball

Baseball

Auto Racing

Golf

Figure Skating

Ice Hockey

Soccer

Tennis

Boxing

a four-year college. Working at a sports summer camp is a great job while you are in college. Meals and lodging are free and you can earn up to $2,500 for the summer. Armed with a diploma, you can get a job as a physical education teacher in an elementary, middle, or high school and can develop sports teams as part of the program. You may even hire outside coaches for these teams. Coaches for scholastic sports teams should all have bachelor's degrees.

The outlook for coaching is very good as a part-time job. Many children play a variety of competitive team and individual sports and they are starting to play from a younger and younger age. To make a full-time career out of the sport you love, consider getting some experience coaching and continue working while you go to college. With coaching experience, good recommendations, and a degree, you should be able to find a teaching position at an elementary-, middle-, or high-school level.

FOR MORE INFORMATION

ORGANIZATIONS

American Alliance for Health, Physical Education, Recreation and Dance (AAHPERD)
1900 Association Drive
Reston, VA 20191
(800) 213-7193 ext. 410
Web site: http://www.aahperd.org
This association is dedicated to increasing awareness about sports and physical education. Publishes several journals and a book on national coaching standards.

National Alliance for Youth Sports (NAYS)
2050 Vista Parkway
West Palm Beach, FL 33441
(561) 684-1141
(800) 729-2057
Web site: http://www.nays.org
This organization has developed a national education program for volunteer youth sport coaches and has also established a code of ethics. Publishes one journal.

National Council for Accreditation of Coaching Education (NCACE)
C/O NASPE
1900 Association Drive
Reston, VA 20191
(703) 476-3417
e-mail: cbolger@aahperd.org
This new organization is concerned with accrediting existing coaching education programs according to national standards. It is the first of its kind.

National Youth Sports Safety Foundation
333 Longwood Avenue, Suite 202
Boston, MA 02115
(617) 277-1171
Web site: http://www.nyssf.org
This organization focuses on reducing the number and severity of injuries while promoting sports and fitness in youth.

BOOKS

Bradley, Bill. *Values of the Game*. New York: Artisan, 1998.

Cross, Neville R., and John Lyle. *The Coaching Process: Principles and Practice*. Woburn, MA: Butterworth-Heinemann, 1999.

Hudson, Frederic M. *Handbook of Coaching*. San Francisco: Joosey-Bass, 1999.

Pryor, Karen. *Don't Shoot the Dog: The New Art of Teaching and Training*. New York: Bantam Books, 1999.

Thompson, Jim. *Positive Coaching: Building Character and Self-Esteem Through Sports*. Portola Valley, CA: Warde Publishers, 1995.

7

YOGA
TEACHER

Yoga is hot. It's in. It's what everyone from five to ninety-five is talking about and doing. People practice yoga to become physically fit and flexible, to relieve stress, to meditate and discover inner spirituality, and ultimately to promote the union of body and mind. In fact the word "yoga," which comes from ancient Sanskrit,

70

means "union." Yoga comes from India and has been around for 5,000 years. Relatively new in the United States, there are currently 15 million Americans who practice some form of yoga, and 75 percent of U.S. health clubs offer yoga classes.

There are eight branches of yoga. The common goal is the search for enlightenment. If you are doing yoga in America, chances are you are practicing some form of hatha or physical yoga. This is the yoga of postures and breathing techniques. Iyengar yoga concentrates on bending the joints and uses props such as cushions, blocks, and straps for students who are not flexible. The founder, B. K. S. Iyengar, has trained thousands of teachers in his style. Kripalu yoga is divided into three stages: learning the postures, holding the postures, and connecting them into a meditation in motion. Kundalini yoga combines postures, chanting, breath control, and meditation. The Healthy, Happy, Holy Organization (3HO), is the home of Kundalini yoga in Los Angeles, but has branches around the world. In Ashtanga yoga, or power yoga, students hop quickly between postures to promote stamina and flexibility. Jivamukti is much like Ashtanga and includes spiritual teaching. It is very popular with celebrities like Madonna and Christy Turlington. Bikram yoga is known as "hot and sweaty" yoga. Often the thermostat is kept at more than 100 degrees in the practice room. Bikram

Choudhury teaches in Beverly Hills, California, and he must certify any teacher of Bikram yoga. Integral yoga combines the body, mind, and spirit through postures, correct breathing, relaxation, and meditation. Yoga is used by physical therapists for joint rehabilitation and by doctors to lower cholesterol levels and blood pressure, among other things.

Before you start training to teach yoga, you must decide which style or styles are right for you. Many people today are coming up with a mix of styles. It's important to have good, formal teacher training. People train directly with gurus, or with the guru's disciples. There are many good retreats or ashrams you can go to for intensive, four-week programs. Not only are you learning teaching skills, you are living a yogic lifestyle in a yogic community. A list of these communities appears in the directory of this chapter.

Yoga teachers are needed in fitness centers, YMCAs, and yoga schools. Some corporations have on-site yoga teachers. Even after-school programs are hiring yoga teachers to teach yoga to kids. Many institutions require a certain number of training hours before they will hire you.

People practice yoga to become physically fit, improve flexibility, and discover inner spirituality.

This photo shows a session of the morning yoga program *Inhale* on Oxygen TV, a cable channel.

The Yoga Alliance, a group of yoga instructors who have completed a certified program with a minimum of 200 hours of study, will register you on their Web site with the initials R.Y.T. (registered yoga teacher) 200 (or 500, depending on the number of hours you have trained) next to your name. This helps to promote you as a yoga teacher. Any training program you have completed, along with certifications, should of course appear on your résumé.

Once you have established yourself as a yoga teacher, you will try to get as many students as you can to make your

Terminology

Many people who practice yoga add Sanskrit words to their everyday vocabulary. Sanskrit is the ancient sacred or scholarly language of India. "Om" is the basic vibrational sound and is the most sacred. It comprises the sounds "ah," "ooh," and "mmm." *Om Shanthi* means "peace." When teachers say *Namaste* or *J'ai bhagwan* at the end of a class they are saying "I honor the light within you."

class economically successful. You may be teaching a class at a big gym, but if only a few people show up, you won't make any money. Putting up notices in health food stores or pharmacies is an excellent way to advertise. These two sites attract people who seek to live healthier, more holistic lifestyles. Private lessons can pay well since some people enjoy having teachers come to their home.

A yoga teacher should set an example for a yogic lifestyle. He or she should be skilled in postures, yet be considerate of others who may not be as flexible. At no time should a teacher force a student to go beyond his or her comfort zone or express any personal judgments about the student's abilities.

A beginning yoga instructor can earn from $20 to $30 an hour working for someone else. Once you establish your reputation, you can charge up to $100 or more depending on your level of demand. The outlook for this career is very good since the number of people doing yoga has doubled in the past five years.

FOR MORE INFORMATION

ORGANIZATIONS

Iyengar Yoga Institute of San Francisco
2404 27th Avenue
San Francisco, CA 94116
(415) 753-0909
Web site: http://www.iyisf.org
Daily classes, retreats, and a teacher training program.

Kripalu
P.O. Box 793
Lenox, MA 01240
(413) 448-3152
(800) 741-7353
Web site: http://www.kripalu.org
Offers daily workshops, week-long programs, and month-long training.

Satchidananda Ashram—Yogaville
Route 1, Box 1720
Buckingham, VA 23921
(434) 969-3121
(800) 858-YOGA (9642)
Web site: http://www.yogaville.org
Integral yoga-based. Has centers in San Francisco and New York City that offer a four-week teacher training program.

Unity Woods Yoga Center
4853 Cordell Avenue, Suite PH7
Bethesda, MD 20814-3036
(301) 656-8992
Web site: http://www.unitywoods.com
The largest Iyengar yoga center in the United States. Classes for teens, pregnant women, people with heart problems, and others. Offers a teacher training course.

Yoga Alliance
(877) 964-2255
Web site: http://www.yogaalliance.org
A voluntary group of different yoga organizations and individual yoga teachers with the mission of providing support for them.

WEB SITES

Yoga Site
http://www.yogasite.com
This Web site has a national listing of yoga teachers and a link to teacher training.

BOOKS

Birch, Beryl Bender. *Power Yoga: The Total Strength and Flexibility Workout.* New York: Simon & Schuster, 1995.

Christensen, Alice. *The American Yoga Association Beginner's Manual.* New York: Fireside Books, 1987.

Iyengar, B. K. S. *Light on Yoga.* New York: Schocken Books, 1979.

Pierce, Margaret, and Martin Pierce. *Yoga for Your Life: A Practice Manual of Breath and Movement for Every Body.* Portland, OR: Rudra Press, 1996.

MAGAZINES
Yoga Journal
A very well-respected bimonthly magazine devoted to yoga.

8

TEACHING BEYOND THE BOUNDARIES

Once you become skilled at a movement technique, you can adapt it for a special clientele. Do you like working with very young children, with families, or with seniors? There are plenty of opportunities out there, and with a little creativity you can develop some of your own.

There are numerous play and music organizations that exist

nationwide whose mission it is to engage babies and very young children in movement and music. Many of these companies have set syllabi or lessons that the teachers must follow. Owners look for energetic individuals who are friendly and love kids. They should be able to move well and handle apparatus such as floor parachutes, children's play equipment, musical instruments, bubble-making devices, and simple puppets. Singing is often part of the class, so being able to carry a tune helps. In some music-oriented programs, you need to play the guitar or some other musical instrument. You must be a good leader and show caregivers how to use the equipment with their babies. Most of these places have a training program that educates you in their methodology.

Creative movement classes are the bridge between "mommy and me" classes and real dance classes for nursery school–aged kids. These children are usually between three and six years old. Classes use movements that prepare the future dancer for formal dance training. Students sit in a circle where everyone can see the teacher and create butterflies, flying saucers, and flowers with their bodies. The children's imaginations are called upon extensively as they assign colors

Young boys practice climbing at the University of Idaho Climbing Center in Moscow, Idaho.

A group of young women participate in an "expressive therapy" class at the Lesley University in Cambridge, Massachussets.

to different dance objects, use props such as scarves and drums, and act out stories to music. Bring as many props and ideas to class as you can think of. Different children will interpret an old trunk full of clothes in many different ways.

Yoga classes exist for pregnant women, postpartum women, and even new moms and their babies. Hospital programs also teach baby massage, which you can work into your postpartum yoga class.

If fitness is more your thing, observe some mommy and me classes and try to work some of the toddler songs and routines into your calisthenics, stretch, body conditioning, breathing, and relaxation routines. You can recommend using the baby as a weight to get back into shape. The baby sits on the pelvis, shins, or arms, depending on what part of the body Mom is working. Colorful scarves can be attached to weights to entertain baby.

You may also want to teach a special yoga or fitness class for seniors. Special clinics are available under various certification programs to guide you with active older-adult activities and exercise choices for people with limitations.

Dance classes can also be modified for seniors. Social and folk-dancing classes are very popular among this age group.

As dance becomes increasingly popular on the elementary and the secondary level, there is more demand for dance educators. College students are combining their education and dance degrees and someone is needed to teach these future teachers. Many colleges and universities will grant waivers or equivalencies based on real-life experience. If you've danced with a ballet company for seven years, some colleges may grant you "equivalent professional experience." Although you can come in at a full-time level as an assistant professor, you will be limited in terms of promotion if you do not go to college. The good news is that you may be granted a certain amount of time to finish your degree while you are working and may be placed on a tenured track. Tenure is a

Mommy and Me Teacher

Dancer Liz Schneider decided to put her old and new skills to use after her first son was born. She borrowed from her dance background and added techniques she learned in her parenting classes to start a "shape up with baby" class at the 92nd Street YWHA in New York. In the class, moms use their babies as weights to exercise abdominal, thigh, and arm muscles. Babies are entertained as moms wave colorful scarves to rhythmic movement. Over the years, Liz has become certified in aerobics and her classes have shifted accordingly. "Women want the aerobics," says Liz. This popular class is in its fifteenth year.

desirable position since it virtually guarantees you employment at the institution. A full-time position pays anywhere from $25,000 to $55,000 a year as a starting salary. A full load is considered three courses a semester.

It's also possible to get work on a part-time basis. Adjunct professors usually earn $2,000 a course. Choreographing a show is another way to get your foot in the door. Often the time spent rehearsing a show is considered a course, and you are paid accordingly.

FOR MORE INFORMATION

ORGANIZATIONS

American Ballroom Theater
25 West 31st Street
Fourth Floor
New York, NY 10001
(212) 244-9442
Web site: http://www.americanballroomtheater.com
This organization will train you to teach ballroom dancing to all ages, including seniors.

Golden Bridge
5901 West 3rd Street
Los Angeles, CA
(323) 936-4172
Web site: http://www.goldenbridge.com
The internationally known guru Gurmuhk conducts a certification course for teaching mothers and babies.

Gymboree
(877) 449-6933
Web site: http://www.gymboree.com
Highly successful play and music classes. Instructors should have movement and some musical ability, energy, creativity, and a love for children. Over 400 franchises worldwide including Canada. Hiring and training are done by local franchises so check online or in your local phone book for the one nearest you.

HealthCare Dimensions
335 Manitou Avenue
Manitou Springs, CO 80829
(800) 373-3401
Web site: http://www.healthcaredimensions.com
This company administers a senior-fitness program called Silver
Sneakers and trains instructors.

Kindermusik International, Inc.
P.O. Box 26575
Greensboro, NC 27415
(888) 442-4453
(336) 273-5154
Web site: http://www.kindermusic.com
An international early childhood music and movement program from
birth through age seven, which stresses that every child is musical.
You can be an instructor even if you do not play a musical instrument.

Kripalu
P.O. Box 793
Lenox, MA 01240
(800) 741-7353
(413) 448-3152
Web site: http://www.kripalu.org
This center has a special workshop on pre- and postpartum yoga.

Music Together
66 Witherspoon Avenue
Princeton, NJ 08542
(800) 728-2692
Web site: http://www.musictogether.com
An international early childhood music and movement program for
all ages, newborn through five.

BOOKS

Francina, Suza. *The New Yoga for People Over 50*. Deerfield Beach, FL: Health Communications, 1997.

Golden, Manine Rosa. *Shall We Dance? Eight Classic Ballroom Dances in Eight Quick Lessons*. New York: Hyperion, 1997.

Jordan, Sondra. *Yoga for Pregnancy: Safe and Gentle Stretches*. New York: St. Martin's Press, 1987.

Levy, Janine. *The Baby Exercise Book*. New York: Pantheon Books, 1975.

9

MARTIAL ARTS INSTRUCTOR

All across the United States people are practicing martial arts. Originally used for self-defense, the martial arts today are studied more as a system of physical and mental conditioning. Students of the martial arts describe an increase in self-discipline, self-confidence, and physical fitness upon practicing and mastering martial arts techniques. Proper breathing techniques are also learned. The martial arts are a wonderful way for young people to learn respect and discipline, something they may not be getting on a daily basis at home or in school.

There are dozens of types of martial arts from countries including China, Japan, Korea, Thailand, Myanmar (Burma), Indonesia, Vietnam, and Cambodia. Some argue that the oldest martial arts come from China, dating from thousands of years ago. There are several hundred forms of Chinese kung fu, a phrase meaning "well done." One popular form practiced these days is tai chi. The movements in tai chi are slow, flowing, and continuous.

Japan's popular arts include judo and karate. Judo, meaning "compliant way," uses grappling techniques, which include locks, holds, and throws. Judo is one of two Olympic martial arts. Karate means "empty hand." This system uses high kicks and energetic punches. In both judo and karate, people graduate into more difficult grades, or *kyu*, according to a system of colored belts. In karate the lowest kyu is the red belt. Then come the white, yellow, orange, green, purple, three grades of brown, and black belts. The black belt is the highest, and there are ten stages of black belt, known as *dans*.

Tae kwon do developed in Korea in the mid-1900s. This "way of the foot and fist" technique borrows a lot from Japanese karate, although the kicks tend to be even higher.

Students participate in a martial arts class at the University of
California at Los Angeles.

Junior high school students compete in a tournament for their local tae kwon do academy in Seoul, Korea.

The World Taekwondo Federation oversees all competitions, including the Olympics. Tae kwon do became an Olympic sport at the Olympic Games in Sydney in 2000.

Although people tend to think of the martial arts as systems of weaponless self-defense, some of the martial arts do use weapons. Kendo, meaning "the way of the sword," uses bamboo swords and began in Japan more than 600 years ago.

In martial arts competitions, contestants perform a series of exercises both alone and with partners. In the form, or *kata*, the student performs a set of movements for aesthetic quality and technical accuracy. Semi-sparring resembles actual fighting, but the moves are prearranged like a choreographed dance. Free-form sparring imitates the unpredictable moves in a real fight.

Experienced masters say it takes from five to ten years of martial arts training to become a good instructor. You can begin martial arts training at any age. Frequently *senseis*, or martial arts masters, will learn several kinds of martial arts to increase the number of students they can accommodate. If a sensei teaches karate, he or she may also teach tai chi chuan. Chances are that younger students will be taking the athletic karate whereas older ones will study the calmer, less physically demanding tai chi chuan. This sensei has used a good marketing strategy, appealing to two distinct groups of people.

The YMCA, a local health club, or a summer youth program are good places to look for a first job as a martial arts teacher. Most martial arts schools are small businesses that can only hire one or two teachers. Opening your own school can be very profitable. Most owners charge monthly fees for taking classes. These range from $50 in a small town to $100 in a larger city with a contract of six months to a year. Private lessons can pay anywhere from $35 to $60. For students to be promoted to the next kyu, they must pass a test, and the owner charges testing fees. Selling uniforms,

A martial arts teacher guides his student through a basic maneuver.

patches of the school or organization, safety equipment, books, and videos also brings in money. You can make additional income by being a judge at competitions. If a competition is held at your school, students pay an entrance fee.

The outlook for teaching martial arts is very good. People are looking for ways to exercise their bodies while they discipline their minds, and the variety of martial arts provides something for everyone. Whether you choose to teach young children in an after-school program or train top-notch students for competition, there is something right for you.

What Are Kyu and Dans?

Dans are the grades of black belt and kyu are the grades of ability below the black belt in the Japanese martial arts. There are nine kyu in karate and six in judo. Colors can vary by school but the most common karate kyu from lowest to highest, after the basic red belt, are:

- *Rokkyu*, or white belt
- *Gokyu*, or yellow belt
- *Shikyu*, or orange belt
- *Sankyu*, or green belt
- *Nikyu*, or blue belt
- Three levels of *Ikkyu*, or brown belt

The level of black belt is divided into sublevels called dans. Depending on the style, the number of dan grades varies from five to twelve. The highest level is usually reserved for the founder of a style or school. Tae kwon do has its own set of grades and belt colors, called keup in Korean.

FOR MORE INFORMATION

ORGANIZATIONS

United Taekwondo International
4707 48th Street, 2nd floor
Camrose, AL T4V 1L2
Canada
A good resource for Canadian tae kwon do.

USA Karate Federation
1300 Kenmore Boulevard
Akron, OH 44314
(330) 753-3114
Web site: http://www.usakarate.org
This group holds classes, certifies instructors, and organizes competitions.

World Martial Arts Association
P.O. Box 1568
Santa Barbara, CA 93102
(805) 569-1389
This group promotes and teaches several martial arts including judo and karate.

WEB SITES

Fighting Arts
http://www.fightingarts.com
Devoted to martial arts enthusiasts. Articles, interviews, and other tidbits of useful information.

Judo Information Site

http://www.judoinfo.com

Check out this Web site for information on techniques, training, competition, and supplies.

Southern California Judo Black Belt Association

http://www.usajudo.com

This Web site is a useful source of information about studios and competitions in the area.

BOOKS

Draeger, Donn F., and Robert W. Smith. *Comprehensive Asian Fighting Arts*. Tokyo: Kodansha International, 1980.

Frederic, Louis. *A Dictionary of Martial Arts*. Boston: Charles Tuttle, 1998.

Goodman, Fay. *The Ultimate Book of Martial Arts*. New York: Lorenz Books, 1998.

Metil, Luana, and Jace Townsend. *Story of Karate: From Buddhism to Bruce Lee* (Lerner's Sports Legacy Series). Minneapolis: Lerner Publications, 1995.

Pedro, Jimmy, et al. *Judo Techniques and Tactics* (Martial Arts Series). Champaign, IL: Human Kinetics, 2001.

Yates, Keith, and H. Bryan Robbins. *Tae Kwon Do Basics*. New York: Sterling Publishing Company, 1987.

10

PILATES INSTRUCTOR

Joseph Pilates (pih-LAH-teez) invented his body-conditioning method at the turn of the twentieth century. His goal was to find a way of exercising the body without stress while forming a relationship between body, mind, and spirit. He achieved this by developing a series of more than 500 movements, using five different pieces of apparatus.

"Contrology" is the name Pilates gave to this system of physical and mental well-being. Instructors in the Pilates technique say their students notice a difference rather quickly, in a matter of weeks. Much of the work is concentrated in the area of the body called "the Powerhouse," namely the abdomen, lower back, and buttocks. Since most of the movements are done with few repetitions, strength is increased without the body-building bulk. Muscles are lengthened, posture is corrected, and tissue damage is helped to heal. Many fitness instructors now incorporate Pilates in their routines, and physical therapists use certain isolated exercises and modified apparatus to help patients. The six basic principles of the Pilates method are concentration, control, centering, flowing movement, precision, and breathing.

Because Pilates was known, even in its early days, to be a corrective measure for posture and injuries, it's not surprising to learn that athletic trainers and choreographers were among the first to recommend Pilates to their athletes and dancers. George Balanchine and Martha Graham sent many dancers for training in Pilates. Romana Kryzanowska, the only living disciple of Joseph Pilates, was originally a Balanchine dancer. Although Pilates was initially not a widely known discipline, today it is in such demand that the Pilates Studio cannot train instructors fast enough. If you opt for a career as a Pilates instructor you can almost certainly

Pilates resistance exercises, designed to build muscle strength, often make use of exercise or weight-training equipment.

find a job at the Pilates studio where you trained, or find a studio that needs a certified instructor, or open your own business! Pilates has become such a hot field that in certain locations there are waiting lists for instruction. If a studio owner who works alone has a waiting list and takes on an associate, he or she can double the clientele!

There is some controversy over Pilates instruction and instructor training. The term "Pilates" recently lost its registered trademark. It is possible to find good instruction and instructor training at studios that are not part of the official

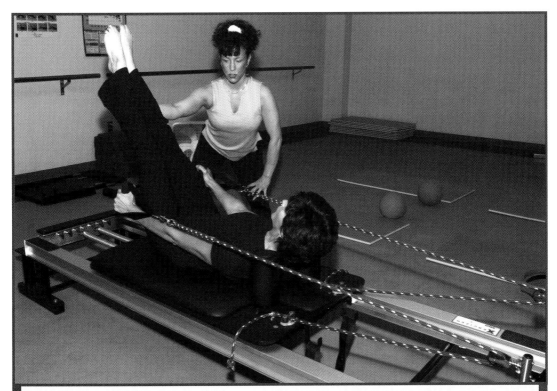

A Pilates instructor guides her client, also a personal trainer, through an exercise routine. The Pilates exercising system is gaining popularity in health clubs as an alternative to conventional exercise.

Pilates Studio. The official studio is run by direct descendants of Joseph Pilates and has centers all over the world. Although you can become certified to teach Pilates by a number of organizations, die-hards argue that the Pilates Studio is the most complete and in-depth training center.

To train at the Pilates Studio, you must log seventy-five hours of class-time instruction yourself so you get a hands-on view of what it's all about. Then you can fill out the application for the teacher certification program. The commitment is intense. Each session costs anywhere from

$50 to $100. So before you fill out the application for the program, you've spent anywhere from $3,750 to $7,500!

Once you have completed your seventy-five class hours and you decide that you would like to go for certification, you must fill out an application form. A practical assessment test is given by the director of the center. During this assessment you will have to move equipment around and show your knowledge of different movements. Tuition for the program is $3,200 plus the cost of ten private sessions. Once you are accepted into the course you will complete seminar training and an apprenticeship. The two are done simultaneously. The seminars cover beginner, intermediate, and advanced work, and all the different apparatus. There are three ways to participate in seminars: weekend workshops, week-long sessions, and a twelve-consecutive-day intensive course. There are three phases of apprenticeship, each lasting 200 hours for a total of 600 hours. An exam is given at the end of each phase. During the third phase, you can earn an hourly wage since you will be teaching by yourself under supervision.

Once you become a certified Pilates instructor you are eligible to join the Pilates Guild, a support network of certified Pilates instructors. As a member, your name is posted on the Pilates Studio Web site and is given out to prospective students on the 800 number. Membership in the guild is $110 a year.

Once you start working as a certified Pilates instructor you can expect to earn anywhere from $20 to $100 an hour. If you work for yourself you will obviously earn more than if you work for a studio, which will only give you a portion of what it charges. But if you do work for yourself you must invest in a lot of expensive equipment. Ideally you should work for someone when you start your career to learn about the business and then, when you are ready, branch out on your own.

Ever wonder why these stars look so good at the Academy Awards?

- Kate Hudson
- Courtney Cox
- Patrick Swayze
- Melanie Griffith
- Danny Glover

Hint: They all do Pilates!

Kate Hudson

FOR MORE INFORMATION

ORGANIZATIONS

The Physicalmind Institute
1807 Second Street, Suite 40
Santa Fe, NM 87505
Web site: http://www.themethodpilates.com
(505) 988-1990
(800) 505-1990
The Web site is sponsored by an alternate training facility and offers their view and training qualifications in Pilates.

Pilates Studio
890 Broadway
6th Floor
New York, NY 10003
(800) 474-5283
Web site: http://www.pilates-studio.com
More information on Pilates, a list of certified instructors, and a list of certifying centers

WEB SITES

Balanced Body
http://www.pilates.com

The Pilates Studio
http://www.pilates-studio.com

BOOKS

Gallagher, Sean P., and Romana Kryzanowska. *The Pilates Method of Body Conditioning*. Philadelphia: BainBridge Books, 1999.

Siler, Brooke. *The Pilates Body*. New York: Broadway Books, 2000.

Winsor, Mari, and Mark Laska. *The Pilates Powerhouse*. New York: Perseus Books, 1999.

11

FELDENKRAIS PRACTITIONER

If you enjoy working with people to help them overcome limitations, teaching the Feldenkrais (FELD-en-crise) method could be just for you. Feldenkrais is fast becoming a very popular way to teach movement. The goal is to enhance physical and mental capabilities through various exercises. As the student becomes more aware of his or her movements, he or she learns to expand the range of physical and mental capabilities. As a Feldenkrais practitioner, you can choose to work with a variety of people. You may choose to work with people who suffer from chronic pain or physical limitations such as arthritis, stroke damage, or cerebral palsy. Feldenkrais cannot reverse the effects of these conditions, but it can teach the student how to maximize functioning by becoming more aware of how his or her body moves. Other students of Feldenkrais include actors, musicians, and dancers. Learning how to maximize functioning of the body will help improve performance for these individuals. People who work at desk jobs or people who are on their feet all day long can benefit from the Feldenkrais method as well. How many times do you hear people bellyache about how their backs hurt or how stressed out they are? By observing how one moves and by learning to move in an efficient way, people lessen these effects of everyday living.

There are two major ways you can teach Feldenkrais: in a group setting or one-on-one. Awareness Through Movement lessons are made up from the hundreds of exercises developed by the founder, Moshe Feldenkrais. The teacher guides the students through a sequence of movements while the students are lying on the floor, standing, or sitting on the floor or in a chair. The movements may seem very simple. The goal is not to be an Olympic athlete.

Feldenkrais methods are designed to enhance physical and mental capabilities through exercise.

Rather, Olympic athletes use Feldenkrais to maximize their potential. Often Feldenkrais students say they feel more relaxed, less stressed, and better able to perform at whatever they do. Functional Integration is a one-to-one learning process in which the practitioner gently places his or her hands on the student's body and guides that student through a series of movements creating greater self-awareness and making way for new and less harmful physical movements. Feldenkrais practitioners believe that a greater awareness of healthier physical movement will lead to new paths created in the mind for one to remember and recreate these new movements.

A Feldenkrais practitioner must go through 800 to 1,000 hours of approved training at one of many recognized sites in order to become accredited. This process usually takes four years. A student associate need complete only two years of training and is certified to teach Awareness Through Movement classes. There are many places to become certified in this country and around the world. You will find information on where these places are located at the end of the chapter.

Once you become a certified Feldenkrais practitioner you will decide how you want to practice. Do you want to work for yourself or for someone else? Do you want to teach groups of people in Awareness Through Movement classes or is one–on-one your thing? Fees per student for group lessons range anywhere from $10 to $15 per class. The amount you earn per class will depend on how many students you have. Some practitioners have open-ended, ongoing classes. Others find it useful to sign people up for a once-a-week, six-week session. For a one-to-one session, starting fees today are $50 and can go as high as $100 or more. The outlook is good for Feldenkrais practitioners. People's interest in health, fitness, and alternative ways to heal is high.

Feldenkrais practitioners believe that proper exercise of the body can focus the mind.

The Feldenkrais method was developed in the late 1940s by Moshe Feldenkrais. Originally an engineer and a physicist, he became interested in judo and was the first European to earn a black belt. He taught himself to walk again after a severe knee injury and was convinced that the movement of the body could influence the mind.

Step one is to take a Feldenkrais class yourself and see if it works for you. You can do this by finding someone in your area through the official Web site listed below.

Suzanne Toren, Feldenkrais practitioner, says:

"Coming from an acting background, I was naturally drawn to working with actors. Often actors are stuck moving one way or moving and then talking. When I get them to discover and become aware of the infinite possibilities of the ways their bodies can move, they become more versatile and frequently find more jobs."

FOR MORE INFORMATION

ORGANIZATIONS

Feldenkrais Guild of North America
3611 SW Hood Avenue, Suite 100
Portland, OR 97201
(800) 775-2118
(503) 221-6612
Web site: http://www.feldenkrais.com
Information and history of Feldenkrais. Also includes a listing of practitioners in your area.

BOOKS

Alon, Ruthy. *Mindful Spontaneity: Lessons in the Feldenkrais Method*. Berkeley, CA: North Atlantic Books, 1996.

Feldenkrais, Moshe. *Body and Mature Behavior.* New York: Harper & Row, 1972.

Feldenkrais, Moshe. *Awareness Through Movement*. New York: Harper & Row, 1977.

Feldenkrais, Moshe. *The Case of Nora*. New York: Harper & Row, 1977.

12

ALEXANDER TECHNIQUE TEACHER

Alexander Technique can be taught one-on-one or in a classroom format. It's been around for more than 100 years and like some of the other practices that combine body, mind, and spirit, it has reached quite a popular level of demand right now.

Students come to learn Alexander Technique in order to alleviate pain, to relieve stress, and to use their bodies in a more efficient way. There are no set exercises and the only apparatus is the teaching table. A large mirror is used so the student can observe himself or herself, and a space large enough to move around in is essential. Many teachers give classes privately in homes.

The class may start the minute a student walks into the room. The teacher observes how he takes off his coat, how he bends over to put it on the chair, and if he slumps once he sits down. The work is done lying down, sitting, or standing. As the teacher observes where the student is feeling tension, he or she lays hands on that area of the body and physically demonstrates how to release the tension and move in a more appropriate way. A good Alexander Technique teacher uses his or her body in the same way he or she instructs the student to. Students can range in age from eight to ninety-eight. A student with emphysema may use Alexander Technique to take pressure off her lungs. Another may take classes because he wants to perform better in athletic events and onstage.

Alexander Technique work centers on releasing unnecessary muscle tension. Frederick Matthias Alexander, an

Alexander Technique is popular among track-and-field athletes and their coaches.

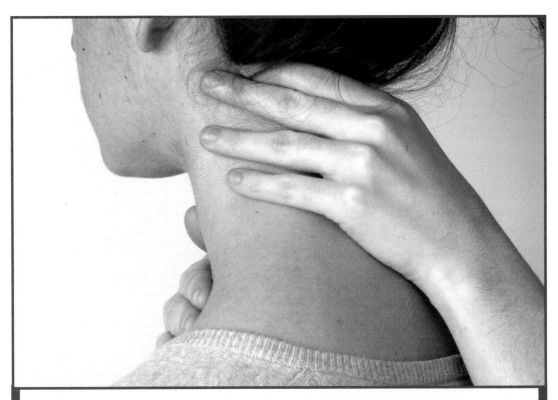

An instructor in Alexander Technique works to relieve a client's muscle tension.

Australian Shakespearian orator with recurring voice problems, discovered that by changing his posture and breathing, he could correct his loss of voice. By studying habits on his own body, he came to realize that much of the movement that is counterproductive to our bodies is learned early in life. The Alexander Technique is about unlearning bad habits that have taken years to develop. Students find new, healthier ways of doing everyday tasks. They are shown ways of sitting, standing, and walking that put less strain on their muscles and joints.

Separating the head from the spine is an important concept in Alexander Technique. When the head balances correctly at the top of the spine, the rest of the body becomes free to move in a coordinated manner, free from compression. Alexander Technique uses tremendous powers of observation. In group classes, students watch each other and comment on each other's posture and movement. In a private class, the teacher observes the student and then applies touch to correct areas of tension gently. The mirror is extremely valuable in showing the student how to observe himself or herself. Ultimately the student should be able to make the adjustment without the teacher. An Alexander Technique teacher coaches the student in three things: awareness, inhibition, and direction. The student learns to be aware of what he or she does and learns to consciously inhibit the misuse of his or her body. Finally he or she tunes into the natural way the body is meant to be used.

It takes three years—approximately 1,500 hours of study—to become a certified Alexander Technique teacher. Once you have completed a course of study, you can join one of the Alexander Technique professional societies and your name will be placed on the Internet and given out over 800 numbers as a referral. Some teachers put in apprenticeship hours rather than do the full training course. In these cases, a peer-review process allows these teachers to become certified. Some teachers choose not to

Alexander Technique and the Performing Arts

Many fine acting schools and music conservatories have Alexander Technique instructors on their staffs. Some of these include:

- The American Dance Festival
- The Julliard School
- The Los Angeles Philharmonic
- The New England Conservatory of Music
- The Royal Academy of Dramatic Art in London

become certified. There is no legal requirement to be certified but you will not receive help with marketing or be on the referral list unless you are certified.

As a teacher of the Alexander Technique, you can work in your home, at a health club, or even as part of a theater club. Depending on your geographical location, you will probably earn about $20 for a forty-five-minute class at a club, or $50 to $100 from your private clients. The outlook for work in this field is good since more and more people are looking to improve the quality of their lives through body-mind techniques.

FOR MORE INFORMATION

ORGANIZATIONS

American Center for the Alexander Technique
39 West 14th Street, Room 507
New York, NY 10011
(212) 633-2229
The oldest Alexander technique training center in the United States.

American Society for the Alexander Technique (AmSAT)
P.O. Box 60008
Florence, MA 01062
(800) 473-0620
(413) 584 2359
Web site: http://www.alexandertech.com
AmSAT certifies training courses in the United States. This society can also help you with marketing by putting you on their Web site and giving your name out as a referral.

Canadian Society of Teachers of the Alexander Technique (CANSTAT)
465 Wilson Avenue
Toronto, ON M3H 1T9
Canada
(877) 598-8879
Web site: http://www.canstat.ca
Certifies teacher training courses in Canada. This society can also help you with marketing by putting you on their Web site and giving your name out as a referral.

WEB SITES

Complete Guide to Alexander Technique
http://www.alexandertechnique.com
Web site for further background information, finding a teacher, finding training courses, sample lessons, videos, teacher resources, etc.

BOOKS

Gelb, Michael, and Laura Huxley. *Body Learning*. New York: Henry Holt & Co., 1995.

Leibowitz, Judith, and Bill Connington. *The Alexander Technique*. New York, Harper & Row, 1991.

MacDonald, Glynn. *The Complete Illustrated Guide to Alexander Technique: A Practical Program for Health, Poise and Fitness*. Boston: Element Books, Inc., 1998

13

CLOWNS AND CIRCUS SKILLS

A clown uses physical movement, costume, makeup, and personality to create a character. Many clowns have more than one character, with changes of clothes, makeup, and body movement. A true performer will always search to find the clown that exists within himself or herself. Clowns can be happy, sad, mischievous, and a

Life as a clown or circus performer usually means a life on the road.

thousand other things, but above all they must entertain. Many avenues of work are open to clowns, including stage performances, traveling circuses, party entertainment, teaching, and hospital services.

A good way to start your career is to travel with a circus or to work as an apprentice with a theater group. The hours can be long and the work demanding but you will learn a lot from your colleagues. Often you are required to help out with the production team. You will be called on to put up the tent and to tear down the show, often on the same day.

A clown entertains children at a birthday party.

You will travel from city to city by circus train. First-year pay with a traveling circus is minimal. Apprentices with the Ringling Bros. and Barnum & Bailey Circus earn $300 a week. After the first year, you can negotiate your salary and, if you are good, get a substantial raise.

It is to your advantage to acquire as many skills as you can. With a character and a costume and a bag of tricks up your sleeve, you can entertain at parties and special events. Large corporations, fund-raising committees, and parents of tiny tots all hire multiskilled clowns to entertain at events.

These clowns mingle with guests, sometimes poking fun at them in a good-natured way. Other forms of interaction include face painting, balloon sculpting, and juggling. It's also possible to work up a performance piece with dialogue. Work is found through agents, and many agents list themselves in the yellow pages under party entertainment. You can also form your own business, advertise in local parenting magazines, and sign on repeat business with corporate clients. Multiskilled party entertainers earn $125 an hour, and a party can last from two to four hours.

If foreign travel is your thing, you can audition for a theater group that performs at European art and theater festivals. The pay is low but it is a great way to see the world. Street entertainers are quite common in European cities such as London, Paris, and Amsterdam, and you earn money by busking, or passing the hat. Since people give what they wish, this is an insecure way to make money and if it rains, you're sunk.

Some clowns earn money by teaching. In addition to work in youth and community centers, health clubs, and dance studios, you can work as a teaching artist in a public

A performer juggles axes as he walks across a tightrope at a Renaissance fair.

school. You will have to develop lesson plans to show what your short- and long-term plans are for the students and how they relate to the classroom curriculum. If you decide you would like to teach clown skills full-time and make teaching your profession, you will have to go to college to earn a bachelor's degree with education credits. The Ringling Bros. and Barnum & Bailey Circus began its own education program in 2000. Children in kindergarten through eighth grade receive forty minutes of educational information before seeing a special two-hour show. Circus skills are used to reinforce a classroom curriculum. Spelling words include "circus" and "hippodrome." Children learn that apparatus are objects in circus acts and measurements are demonstrated with animal weights and heights.

Great personal satisfaction comes from working with sick children. The Big Apple Circus Clown Care Unit has set up programs in hospitals nationally to help kids understand various hospital procedures through parody.

You can study clown and circus skills at one of the big circus schools, by apprenticing with small theater compa-nies, or by taking individual lessons. The San Francisco

A clown and juggler performs on his unicycle for a crowd of children in a park.

Do You Know?

You've probably been to the circus a dozen times, but did you know that there are four basic types of clowns? The boss clown likes to push around others

and is generally seen in the presence of other clowns. The uniquely American tramp clown became popular during the Depression. He has put on his fine clothes to go job hunting but soon they become tattered, and his weary face is dusted with soot. The *auguste*

A tramp clown

clown is a patchwork quilt; his shoes are too large and his clothes are too small. With his red nose, he is the most familiar. The pantomime clown reached world notoriety with French artist Marcel Marceau. His movement is highly specialized. Acts based on Marceau's often uses masks and puppets.

School of Circus Arts and the Ecole Nationale de Cirque in Montreal, Canada, are two respected schools. The Bond Street Theater Company in New York offers circus skills classes from time to time and hires apprentices for the company. Many circus performers can be hired to teach classes.

Circuses have seen a revitalization in the past twenty years. The Big Apple Circus, Cirque de Soleil, and Circus Oz exemplify the "new circus." These circuses combine the skill found in traditional circuses with the drama and theatricality of good acting. New circuses take advantage of modern technology with innovations in lighting, contemporary rock music, and multimedia presentations. To compete in the twenty-first century world of circus, it is to your advantage to study acting, dance, and acrobatics in addition to your circus skills.

FOR MORE INFORMATION

ORGANIZATIONS

Big Apple Circus
505 Eighth Avenue
19th Floor
New York, NY 10018-6505
(212) 268-2500
Web site: http://www.bigapplecircus.org
A very well-respected traveling circus. Call to find out about auditions for troupe and the Clown Care Unit.

Bond Street Theatre
2 Bond Street
New York, NY 10012
(212) 254-4614
Web site: http://www.bondst.org
A twenty-five-year-old theater group specializing in many types of physical theater. They travel frequently to Europe to perform and hire interns for the company. If interested contact them directly.

Ecole Nationale de Cirque
417 Berri Street
Montreal, PQ H2Y 3E1
Canada
(514)982-0859
(In Canada) (800) 267-0859
Web site: http://www.enc.qc.ca
A circus conservatory with a competitive entrance exam. Applicants must have a high school diploma and have knowledge

of dance, gymnastics, theater, and circus arts. Canadian students get a collegial degree at the end of three years. Foreign students get a certificate from the school at the end of two years.

NY Goofs

(212) 591-0028
Web site: http://www.nygoofs.com
A troupe of twelve clowns with a multitude of experience. They host a two-week intensive clown course every summer.

Ringling Bros. and Barnum & Bailey Circus

Talent and Production Department
1313 17th Street East
Palmetto, FL 34221
Web site: http://www.ringling.com
This giant among circuses wants you to mail your portfolio or audition tape to them for possible employment.

San Francisco School of Circus Arts

755 Frederick Street
San Francisco, CA 94117
(415) 759-8123
Web site: http://www.sfcircus.org
A top circus arts school that offers semester-long classes as well as master classes. Applications available online.

BOOKS

Eldredge, Sears. *Mask Improvisation for Actor Training and Performance: The Compelling Image.* Evanston, IL: Northwestern University Press, 1996.

Goldberg, Andy. *Improv Comedy.* Hollywood, CA: Samuel French, 1991.

Horn, Delton. *Comedy Improvisation: Exercises and Technique for Young Actors.* Colorado Springs: Meriwether Publications, 1992.

Lecoq, Jacques, Jean-Gabriel Carasso, Jean-Claude Lallias, and Simon McBurney, translated by David Bradby. *The Moving Body: Teaching Creative Theatre*. New York: Routledge Press, 2001.

Robinson, Davis Rider. *The Physical Comedy Handbook*. Portsmouth, NH: Heinemann, 1999.

GLOSSARY

aerobic exercises Exercises that challenge your heart and lungs.

apparatus Any of the pieces of equipment used for Pilates class, Alexander Technique, or circus skills.

body-mind exercise One of several types of workouts that provide mental relaxation and clarity of thought as well as exercise.

busk To perform for money in the street.

callback The second round of auditions for dance hopefuls. These people have successfully passed a preliminary cut.

cardiopulmonary resuscitation (CPR) Techniques used to start the heart beating again or to restore breathing when there's been a breakdown in functioning.

contract A signed agreement between a producer and a performer, which specifies the terms agreed to by both parties.

enlightenment In yogic terms, getting in touch with your inner self.

extracurricular Outside the normal school day.

headshot A black-and-white glossy photo that, with your résumé, is your calling card to auditions and agents.

negotiate To arrange the terms of a contract, with regard to salary and working conditions.

producer The person who finances and supervises the production of a show or dance concert.

repertoire The stock of pieces that a dance (or an opera or theater) company is prepared to perform.

residuals Payments made to a performer for a filmed or taped film, TV show, or commercial for repeated showings.

résumé A one-page summary of one's work experience and skills.

rounds The door-to-door trek with photo and résumé that performers take to agents' doors.

Sanskrit An ancient language of India and the official language of Hinduism.

sensei A martial arts master or teacher.

showcase A show or dance concert in which the performer does not get paid but from which he or she hopes to get either an agent or future work from his or her appearance.

syllabus An outline of the main subjects of a course of study.

tenured To be guaranteed employment at a university, usually after a certain number of years.

INDEX

U
unions, 28, 39

V
volunteering, 62

W
World Taekwando Federation, 92

Y
yoga, 9
  origins of, 70, 71
  types of, 71, 73

yoga teachers, 70–78
  jobs for, 73, 74–75
  requirements for, 75
  salaries for, 76
  specializations, 82, 83
  training for, 73, 74

About the Author

Nicole Flender graduated from New York's High School of Performing Arts as a dance major. She went on to receive a B.A. from Yale University and an M.A. from New York University. She danced professionally for twelve years and now teaches dance in the New York City public school system. She also writes for national dance magazines. Ms. Flender lives in New York with her husband and two children.

Acknowledgments

I would like to thank the following people for their advice in their areas of expertise and for continuing to share their joy of movement with others: Pio Cabada, Luanne Dietrich, Harry Feiner, Deborah Gladstein, Rob Lok, Liz Schneider, and Suzanne Toren.

Photo Credits

Cover, p. 61, 63, 128 © SuperStock; pp. 11, 13 © Ralph Cowan/FPG International; p. 15 © Paul A. Souders/Corbis; pp. 16–17 © Bob Stern/The Image Works; pp. 24, 26–27 © Martha Swope/TimePix; p. 29 © Everett Collection, Inc.; p. 30 © Marty Lederhandler/AP Wide World Photos; pp. 35, 36 © David H. Wells/Corbis; p. 38 © David Reed/Corbis; pp. 42,

Design and Layout

Evelyn Horovicz